Borderline Personality Disorder

The ultimate guide to borderline personality disorder including signs and symptoms, diagnosis, treatment, and how to improve and manage it!

Copyright 2015

Table of Contents

Introduction 1

Chapter 1: Understanding Borderline Personality Disorder 2

Chapter 2: Treating Borderline Personality Disorder with Psychotherapy 9

Chapter 3: What Medications can you Take for Borderline Personality Disorder? 16

Chapter 4: Alternative Treatments for Borderline Personality Disorder 20

Chapter 5: Naturopathy, Aromatherapy, Rehabilitation, and Hospitalization for Borderline Personality Disorder 25

Conclusion 27

Introduction

I want to thank you and congratulate you for downloading the book, "Borderline Personality Disorder".

This book contains helpful information about Borderline Personality Disorder, what it is, and the signs and symptoms.

While there is no exact cause known of Borderline Personality Disorder, several of the supposed contributing factors are discussed in this book. If you or a loved one have a Personality Disorder, this guide should be able to help you to better understand it.

This book explains the diagnosis process, and explains what factors must be present for it to be confirmed that you do in fact suffer from Borderline Personality Disorder.

This book also includes great tips and techniques that will help you to better understand and improve the disorder. It explains the different treatment options, including the therapies available, drugs that may be prescribed, alternative therapies, and also rehabilitation programs.

This book covers all that you need to know to better understand Borderline Personality Disorder, and begin improving it today!

Thanks again for downloading this book, I hope you enjoy it!

Chapter 1: Understanding Borderline Personality Disorder

Borderline personality disorder is a mental disorder characterized by unstable moods and behavior. Those who have this disorder usually suffer from unstable relationships with other people, reckless and impulsive behavior, and problems with regulating thoughts and emotions.

In addition, those who have this condition tend to have a high risk of suffering from other disorders, such as anxiety disorders, depression, eating disorders and substance abuse, along with suicidal behaviors, suicide attempts, and self-harm. In the United States, around 1.6% of adults have borderline personality disorder.

Symptoms of Borderline Personality Disorder

According to the Diagnostic and Statistical Manual for Mental Disorders, you may be diagnosed with borderline personality disorder if you display a behavioral pattern that includes at least five of these symptoms:

- A pattern of stormy and intense relationships with friends, family and romantic partners. Such relationships usually veer from extreme love and closeness to extreme anger or dislike

- Extreme reactions, including depression, panic, frantic actions and rage, to perceived or real abandonment

- Dangerous and impulsive behaviors, such as substance abuse, binge eating, spending sprees, and reckless driving

- Unstable and distorted sense of self or self-image, which results to sudden changes in opinions, feelings, goals, values, and plans for the future

- Recurring suicidal threats or behaviors, as well as self-harming tendencies, such as cutting

- Chronic feelings of boredom or emptiness

- Highly changeable and intense moods, with every episode lasting from several hours to several days

- Having paranoid thoughts related to stress or highly dissociative symptoms, such as losing touch with reality, observing self from outside of the body, and feeling cut off from self

- Intense and inappropriate anger or problems with managing anger

Note that certain events, no matter how mundane they may seem, might still trigger these symptoms. For instance, those with borderline personality disorder may feel distressed and angry over minor separations, such as business trips, vacations and sudden changes in plans, from the people whom they feel close to.

According to studies, those who have this disorder may also view anger as a neutral emotion and tend to have a stronger reaction towards words that have negative connotations.

Likewise, borderline personality disorder sufferers may harm themselves in order to help regulate their emotions, express their pain, or punish themselves. Unfortunately, they do not see these actions as harmful. About eighty percent of individuals with borderline personality disorder have suicidal behaviors, and four to nine percent of them actually commit suicide.

Causes of Borderline Personality Disorder

There is no single exact cause of borderline personality disorder. The majority of researchers believe that this disorder develops through a combination of factors, such as temperament and experiences during childhood and adolescence. Difficult life events such as physical or sexual abuse, childhood neglect, and early loss of a parent can also contribute to the disorder developing. Those who already have borderline personality disorder can experience worsened symptoms if they encounter a difficult situation, such as loss of a job or a breakup.

When Does Borderline Personality Disorder Begin?

Usually, this disorder starts at adolescence or early adulthood. Many researchers suggest that its early symptoms may even occur during childhood. Some of those who suffer from borderline personality disorder experience severe symptoms and need intensive inpatient care. Nonetheless, there are also patients who may need outpatient care only, not emergency care or hospitalization. In addition, there are people with this disorder who improve without needing any treatment.

What Other Illnesses can Co-Occur with Borderline Personality Disorder?

Certain illnesses can make borderline personality disorder more difficult to diagnose and treat. This is especially true if their symptoms overlap with the symptoms of borderline personality disorder. Nonetheless, women have a higher risk of developing disorders that co-occur with borderline personality disorder. Such disorders include antisocial personality disorder and substance abuse.

Likewise, those with borderline personality disorder may also develop illnesses, such as chronic back pain, high blood pressure, diabetes, fibromyalgia, and arthritis. These conditions are linked to obesity, a common side effect of medications for mental health disorders, including borderline personality disorder.

According to the National Comorbidity Survey Replication, about eighty-five percent of individuals suffering from borderline personality disorder meet the diagnostic criteria for other mental disorders too.

Are there Risk Factors Associated with Borderline Personality Disorder?

According to researchers, certain risk factors may be evident with borderline personality disorder. Environmental factors and genetics, for instance, may contribute to the development of the disorder.

In a study that involved twins, it has been discovered that borderline personality disorder is inherited. In another study, it has been found that individuals can inherit their personality traits and temperament, such as aggression and impulsiveness.

What's more, cultural or social factors may also increase the risk of this disorder. For instance, if you belong to a culture or community wherein unstable family relationships are prevalent, you may have a higher risk of borderline personality disorder.

Poor judgment and impulsiveness along with other consequences of borderline personality disorder may cause you to be in risky situations. You may also be a victim of rape, violence, and other crimes.

Diagnosis of Borderline Personality Disorder

Oftentimes, borderline personality disorder is misdiagnosed or underdiagnosed. Mental health professionals, such as psychiatrists, psychologists, psychiatric nurses, and clinical social workers usually detect this disorder based on discussions and interviews about the symptoms. In addition, a series of thorough and careful medical exams can help them rule out other possible causes of these symptoms.

If you want to confirm if you have borderline personality disorder, you should allow your mental health professional to ask about your medical history. You should inform them about your family and personal histories of mental disorders as well as symptoms. In certain cases, mental disorders that co-occur with borderline personality disorder may have overlapping symptoms. This can make it difficult for your doctor to distinguish borderline personality disorder from the others.

In addition, you should take note that no exact test can diagnose borderline personality disorder. Nonetheless, a study found that adults suffering from borderline personality disorder show excessive emotional reactions whenever they look at words that have unpleasant connotations. Those with a more severe case of the disorder also showed much more intense emotional reactions as compared to individuals with a lesser intensity of borderline personality disorder.

Are there Studies Being Conducted to Improve the Diagnosis of Borderline Personality Disorder?

According to recent neuroimaging studies, the brain structures of individuals with borderline personality disorder and those who do not have it are different. Some researchers suggest that the brain areas involved in emotional reactions become overactive in individuals with borderline personality disorder each time they complete tasks that they view as negative.

Likewise, those with borderline personality disorder show less activity in their brain areas that help regulate aggressive impulses and emotions, as well as let people understand the context of a particular situation. Such findings may help in explaining the explosive and unstable mood characteristics of borderline personality disorder.

In another study, it has been found that people with this disorder used areas of their brain that are different from those who do not have borderline personality disorder. Those who have the disorder used areas of their brain related to alertness and reflective actions. This most probably explains why they have the tendency to respond impulsively on emotional cues.

How About if you Feel that your Diagnosis was Inaccurate?

If you feel that you were only given that diagnosis because you do not easily fit into any other category, you can go and ask for a second opinion. Then again, you should keep in mind that this does not necessarily mean that you can get your request. If you have a hard time obtaining the help that you need, you may search for an advocate or a person who can support and speak up for you.

Chapter 2:
Treating Borderline Personality Disorder with Psychotherapy

Psychotherapy is an approach that involves different types of therapy, such as dialectical behavior therapy, cognitive behavioral therapy, schema-focused therapy, mentalization-based therapy and transference-focused psychotherapy.

Psychotherapy is also commonly used to treat people with borderline personality disorder to help them overcome their issues. It is crucial to keep in mind that even though medications can be a good solution for symptoms, they may have major side effects.

In addition, medications cannot help patients learn emotion regulation, coping skills, and other important skills that they can use to improve their life. In addition, a major objective of psychotherapy is to prevent a person with personality disorder from committing suicide.

It is crucial for suicidality to be assessed and monitored throughout the whole course of treatment. When a person with borderline personality disorder displays severe symptoms, they may need to receive medication or be confined in a hospital for several days. Anyway, the following types of psychotherapy should also be tried before going for a more invasive treatment procedure.

Cognitive Behavioral Therapy

Cognitive behavioral therapy is a treatment method that involves working with a mental health counselor in order to become more aware of negative and inaccurate thinking.

Patients work with a therapist so they can view challenging situations in a more objective manner. In addition, they may work with a therapist so they can learn how to practice alternative solution techniques.

What can you expect from it? This kind of therapy focuses mainly on the present. This means that you should not dwell on your past experiences. You can still explain how you came to behave or think the way you do, but you should focus on how you behave in the present.

Cognitive behavior therapy is directive. You can expect your therapist to be active during your sessions. They will provide you with direct advice. In other kinds of therapies, the therapists just sit back and listen while the patients direct their session.

In addition, in cognitive behavioral therapy, the therapist assumes that your symptoms are connected to the behavioral and thinking patterns that you have adapted throughout the years. Thus, they do not believe that spending one to two hours a week in therapy is sufficient to produce significant results.

They are most likely to give assignments and let the patients work on changing their behavioral and thinking patterns outside of therapy sessions. Before a session ends, assignment sheets and handouts are usually given.

Dialectical Behavior Therapy

Dialectical behavior therapy is specifically designed to treat borderline personality disorder. Generally, it is done via phone counseling, individual sessions and group sessions. It makes use of a skills-based approach combined with meditation and exercises to help patients with borderline personality disorder learn how to regulate their emotions, improve their relationships and tolerate their distress.

During individual therapy, the therapist is the main therapist and the patient undergoes therapy sessions. The patient goes to the office of the therapist to speak about their experiences, thoughts, and feelings among other things.

During telephone contact, the patient speaks to the therapist using the phone in between sessions. You should keep in mind that phone contact is not done for the purpose of psychotherapy though. Instead, it is essential to give the patient support and help so that they may apply the skills that they've learned into real life situations. It is also meant to help them avoid injuring themselves.

Furthermore, the patient may call their therapist if they need to mend any issues between them prior to the next therapy session. Then again, they are not allowed to call within the next twenty-four hours if they injure themselves in order to prevent the reinforcement of self-injury.

Anyway, if you undergo skills training, you will need to talk to a therapist. You will do this in a room full of other people suffering from the same mental disorder. Just like you, these patients are also taught skills that may prove to be useful in daily situations. Such skills include emotion modulation, core mindfulness, distress tolerance, and interpersonal effectiveness.

What are these skills about? Well, emotion modulation skills refer to the skills that help you deal with states of distressing emotion. Core mindfulness skills, on the other hand, are based on Buddhist meditation techniques. However, the religion does not necessarily influence it. You can practice these meditation techniques without having to convert to Buddhism. You can also use them to help you become more aware of your experiences and be able to be mindful of your present.

Distress tolerance skills are about practicing techniques that help you deal with different emotional states. These skills are highly useful if you can no longer change such emotional states. Then, there are interpersonal effectiveness skills that focus on helping you achieve your goals with the help of other people. You will be taught how to get what you want by asking for it. Likewise, you will be taught how to refuse certain offers or requests, improve your self-esteem and maintain relationships.

When you are in your therapist consultation group, your therapist receives dialectical behavior therapy while the members of your group are required to focus. In addition, they are required to provide a formal undertaking to stay in therapy and avoid making negative remarks about the other members of the group.

Schema-Focused Therapy

This type of therapy involves a variety of approaches, including cognitive behavior therapy and emotion-based techniques. Such techniques are meant to help you evaluate repetitive life patterns and themes so you can successfully find ways that you can correct them.

Schema-focused therapy mainly focuses on helping patients change their long-standing and negative self-images by means of writing letters, role-playing, assertiveness training, guided imagery, relaxation, anger management, and exposure to certain situations that tend to induce anxiety.

One of the unique key elements of this therapy is limited re-parenting. This involves helping patients build a secure attachment towards their therapist. Keep in mind that such an attachment is still within the boundaries of a professional relationship. Therapists and patients should know where they stand.

Dr. Joan Farrell, the director of the Schema Therapy Institute Midwest Indianapolis Center, said that many people suffering from borderline personality disorder missed emotional learning when they were young. This made them hesitant to express their emotions and needs.

In addition, these people did not receive adequate validation, which is why they became insecure. In schema-focused therapy, the childhood needs of patients like these are met. The therapist makes sure that the needs of the patients are met by giving them nurturance, setting the necessary limitations, and showing them compassion.

By doing this, the patients are able to become healthier emotionally. In addition, they become autonomous, so that they no longer have to go to their therapist for validation or to have their needs met. They are able to meet their needs on their own and do things by themselves.

Mentalization-Based Therapy

This type of psycho-dynamically oriented psychotherapy enables people with borderline personality disorder to determine and isolate their thoughts and feelings from the thoughts and feelings of the people surrounding them. It also generally focuses on thinking before acting.

People with borderline personality disorder tend to have unstable and intense relationships that cause them to exploit or manipulate other people, although they do it unconsciously. These people are not able to recognize the consequences of their actions towards others.

With the help of mentalization-based therapy, they are able to learn how they can get a clearer grasp of their behaviors and feelings, and then associate them with their mental states.

Many studies show that the capacity for mentalization-based therapy of those with borderline personality disorder is not high enough. It is crucial to keep in mind that this type of treatment is essential in traditional psychotherapy. Its concepts are practiced, reinforced and emphasized within a safe and supportive setting. It is also less directive as compared to cognitive behavior therapy.

Transference-Focused Psychotherapy

Also known as psychodynamic psychotherapy, transference-focused psychotherapy aims to help people with borderline personality disorder understand their emotional and interpersonal hardships through the development of their relationship with their therapist. One of its highly distinguishable features is its psychological structure emphasis on the symptoms of the disorder.

Transference-focused psychotherapy focuses on a deeper psychological setup wherein the mind becomes structured around a fundamental split, which determines a way of understanding oneself better. This fundamental split also identifies your perceptions, as well as any chaotic interpersonal relations and behaviors that cause you to self-destruct.

This type of therapy was based on a mind model in which early affectively charged experiences were built into the psychological structure. When you go through transference-focused psychotherapy, you are taught how to apply your thoughts into your daily life. You also transfer your internal images, attitudes, and beliefs to your therapist.

Through transference-focused psychotherapy, you are also able to work through any distorted images that you have already imposed on the reality. As time goes by, your self-reflection capacity increases and you are able to adapt better to life circumstances. Your symptoms of borderline personality disorder are also reduced.

Now that you have learned about the different types of treatment recommended for people with borderline personality disorder, you should keep in mind that whatever treatment you choose, you should have it in a structured therapeutic setting. In addition, it is crucial for you to have a well-defined boundary prior to the therapy sessions.

Chapter 3:
What Medications can you Take for Borderline Personality Disorder?

Aside from therapy, you can also treat borderline personality disorder with medication. While some people disagree with the use of medications due to their side effects, others approve of them. Dr. Phillip Long actually recommends low dosages of antipsychotic medications to help patients get through their reactive psychoses.

Thus, you can take medication to help yourself feel better. Then again, you should take note that even experts do not agree in using medication for long-term regiments. This is because their episodes tend to be self-limiting and short term. They can also have adverse side effects.

Nonetheless, you can still use low dosages of haloperidol and other high potency neuroleptics to help you organize your thoughts as well as treat psychotic symptoms. Moreover, you should take note that there are cases wherein depression can be treated using neuroleptics.

These medications are recommended to patients who show uncontrollable anger issues. Nevertheless, such medications should only be given in low dosages. They should also be acquired using psychosocial intervention. So what types of medications can you use to treat borderline personality disorder?

Antidepressants

People commonly use these drugs to treat mental disorders, including borderline personality disorder and depression. If your friends and family notice that you display signs of suicidal ideation or intent, you should go to a doctor and ask for a prescription for antidepressants.

Antidepressants are available in different types. For instance, you can get SSRIs or selective serotonin reuptake inhibitors. These drugs work by changing the serotonin in your brain. Some of the most common SSRIs on the market include sertraline, paroxetine, fluoxetine, citalopram, and escitalopram.

You can also use MAOIs or monoamine oxidase inhibitors and tricyclics. Amitriptyline, imipramine, and clomipramine are common examples of tricyclics. MAOIs, on the other hand, are very rarely used these days. They are old types of antidepressants and are often not prescribed to patients because of their severe side effects. Tranylcypromine and phenelzine are examples of this drug.

According to studies, antidepressants can be effective in treating symptoms of borderline personality disorder. For instance, you can use SSRIs to reduce your emotional instability, anger issues, tendencies for self-harm and impulsivity. You can also use MAOIs to reduce your emotional instability.

Then again, using medication can have unpleasant consequences. Some of the side effects that you may experience include loss of appetite, headaches, insomnia, sedation and sexual dysfunction. You may also experience weight gain, heart problems, blurred vision, seizures, and dry mouth.

If you are taking MAOIs, you should also be very careful of what you eat. Cheese, soy sauce, and food products that contain tyramine, for instance, should be avoided because they contain ingredients that may increase your risk of hypertension. MAOIs may also reduce the effectiveness of other medications that you are taking.

Anti-Anxiety Medication

Anxiolytics are anti-anxiety drugs. They are mainly used to treat anxiety and intense agitation caused by borderline personality disorder. According to studies, these drugs can effectively reduce the symptoms of the disorder.

Benzodiazepines are the most commonly used anti-anxiety medication. These include clonazepam, lorazepam, alprazolam, and diazepam. However, you should not use these drugs often because they can be habit-forming. They can make you dependent or addicted. This is especially true if you have a substance abuse problem.

Moreover, benzodiazepines are not ideal to be taken with sedating medications and alcohol. The combination can result in side effects such as fatigue, memory problems, impaired coordination, and sleepiness.

Antipsychotics

These drugs are effective in reducing anxiety, paranoid thinking, impulsivity, and intense anger. They are available in two categories: typical and atypical. Doctors rarely prescribe typical antipsychotics to patients with borderline personality disorder because they can cause severe side effects.

Long-term use of antipsychotics can cause uncontrollable movements of the face, lips, tongue, limbs and fingers. Atypical antipsychotics have less movement-related side effects than typical antipsychotics. Some examples of these drugs include clozapine, olanzapine, risperidone, quietiapine and aripiprazole.

Mood Stabilizers

These drugs can reduce mood shifts, emotion dysregulation and impulsivity symptoms that are associated with borderline personality disorder. Your doctor may prescribe you with anticonvulsants that are helpful in treating seizures and non-convulsant mood stabilizers, which can treat mental disorders.

Take note that the side effects of mood stabilizers generally vary depending on their type. Lithium carbonate, for example, can cause tremors, weight gain, cognitive problems, acne and gastrointestinal problems. In addition, it can affect the kidneys and thyroid gland.

Chapter 4:
Alternative Treatments for Borderline Personality Disorder

Because medications are known to cause unpleasant side effects, many people turn to alternative treatments such as herbal remedies and supplements. Herbal remedies are natural treatments that can be just as effective as traditional medication, only less expensive. Supplements contain ingredients that may reduce symptoms of borderline personality disorder.

What Herbal Remedies are Ideal for Treating Borderline Personality Disorder?

The following are the most recommended herbs that you can use to reduce symptoms of borderline personality disorder. However, before you use any of these herbal remedies, see to it that you consult your doctor. Your doctor may not allow you to use such remedies if you have any allergic reactions or are taking other medications that may interfere with the effectiveness of the treatment.

Yerba Mate

Yerba mate was originally found in Argentina. It is commonly used as a natural mood stabilizer, anti-anxiety treatment, and antidepressant. Young children even receive yerba mate to regulate their mood swings. According to the author John Lust, this herb is also a good stimulant that can improve mood, provide relief from fatigue, and stimulate mental energy.

Kava Kava

Kava kava is ideal for fighting against insomnia, anxiety and fatigue. The National Center for Complementary and Alternative Medicine states that this herb is effective for anxiety disorders, and may work as an alternative for benzodiazepines and tricyclics.

If you are worried that this herb may interfere with your mental alertness, worry no more. However, note that even though kava kava does not interfere with mental health, it may be harmful to the liver. Many health professionals do not recommend the use of kava kava for more than three months. Likewise, they do not recommend it if you are also taking psychotropic drugs.

Valerian Root

This herb is widely popular all over the world due to its healing properties. In fact, it has been labeled as Grandmother Earth's Valium. Many people use the valerian root as a nerve tonic. They also use it to treat a variety of health conditions, such as depression, anxiety, and insomnia.

The valerian is also useful for relieving pain, strain, and tension. It also contains properties that can be beneficial to your brain and nervous system. Then again, this herb is not ideal to be taken with sleeping drugs. If you take it with a sleeping pill, it may interfere with the effectiveness of the pill.

In addition, this herb may cause hallucinations. If you have been diagnosed with borderline personality disorder, you should take the valerian root in low dosages only. You may also put it in your tea. Just make sure that you allot about a two to three week break period.

Chamomile

Chamomile has soothing properties that can improve your mood. According to a clinical study that involved people with anxiety disorders, chamomile is effective in relieving symptoms of such disorders. Moreover, it has been found that chamomile contains chemicals that can naturally treat anxiety without producing unpleasant side effects. A cup of chamomile tea is enough to keep you calm and relaxed.

St. John's Wort

St. John's Wort contains properties that can help your body absorb serotonin better. It also increases the levels of serotonin in your body. St. John's Wort is widely known for its effectiveness in reducing symptoms of numerous mental disorders as well as improving mood.

According to studies, this herb can be just as effective as traditional medications and antidepressants. If you want your symptoms of borderline personality disorder, depression or anxiety to be reduced, you can try using St. John's Wort. However, you should keep in mind that this herb is not advisable to be taken with supplements, SSRIs, and MAOIs, because it might alter their effectiveness.

What Supplements can you Use to Treat Borderline Personality Disorder?

Aside from herbal remedies, you can also use supplements to reduce your symptoms of borderline personality disorder. The following are some of the recommended supplements that you can try:

SAM-e or S-Adenosyl L-Methionine

This supplement is an amino acid that you can find inside your body. It helps produce mood-enhancing neurotransmitters, including serotonin and dopamine. A lot of studies and clinical trials show that this supplement can significantly reduce symptoms of depression. It was also found that you could be in a bad mood if there are not sufficient amounts of SAM-e in your body.

Nevertheless, if you have just begun using this supplement, you should take it in low dosages. You can increase the dosage gradually when your body gets used to the supplement. It is never ideal to take SAM-e in very high dosages as it can increase your risk of manic episodes and insomnia. You can take this supplement on an empty stomach and along with B vitamins.

5-HTP or 5-Hydroxytryptophan

5-HTP is similar to SAM-e in the way that both of them are naturally present in your body. This supplement works by regulating and boosting your serotonin production. It helps alleviate feelings of anxiety and depression. In addition, it helps your system avoid sleep problems, such as insomnia.

Taking 5-HTP before going to bed is ideal because it can help you sleep better. Then again, if you have just begun using this supplement, you should not use more than fifty milligrams. Over time, however, you can increase your dosage to about one hundred milligrams.

DHA or Docosahexaenoic Acid

DHA is an omega-3 fatty acid that you can find in cold-water fish oils. Researchers have found that DHA and lithium have similar properties, but DHA does not have the side effects that lithium has. You can take DHA capsules to improve your borderline personality disorder.

See to it that you read the labels, so you will know if the supplement contains high levels of EPA and low levels of DHA. Experts recommend that people with borderline personality disorder take one hundred or two hundred milligrams of DHA on a daily basis.

Chapter 5:
Naturopathy, Aromatherapy, Rehabilitation, and Hospitalization for Borderline Personality Disorder

It is also possible to treat borderline personality disorder with naturopathy and aromatherapy. In more severe cases, however, rehabilitation and hospitalization may be necessary. You should consult your physician to find out which of these treatment methods is most suitable for your condition. You may also want to check if your insurance policy covers rehabilitation and hospitalization.

Naturopathy

This form of therapy involves the use of nature to reduce symptoms of borderline personality disorder. Naturopaths typically use flowers, leaves, roots, stems, and berries to treat the disorder. Many people believe that natural medicine is effective in treating anxiety and depression, among other symptoms. One good thing about this form of therapy is that it helps patients treat the root cause of their problem, instead of simply alleviating their symptoms.

Aromatherapy

Aromatherapy is widely known for its effectiveness in treating a variety of health conditions. It involves the use of essential oils to help people with borderline personality disorder relax. The scent of such fragrant oils can stimulate the nerve that is directly connected to your brain's limbic area. This limbic area of your brain is the one responsible for your emotions, learning, and memory. The most ideal oils for aromatherapy include pine, lavender, bay, juniper, clary sage, marjoram, and basil.

Rehabilitation

Rehabilitation is recommended for people who have a hard time controlling their symptoms of borderline personality disorder. They are usually referred by their therapists to rehabilitation facilities and are advised to stay there for at least three months or until they show improvement.

These rehabilitation facilities clarify diagnoses by conducting psychological exams. They also determine the needs of the patients as well as provide them with a personalized treatment plan. Patients are evaluated based on their cognitive abilities and personality traits. They also undergo psychological exams to measure their intelligence.

Hospitalization

Usually, hospitalization is the last resort of people with borderline personality disorder. Then again, if you are having a hard time treating your disorder with just therapy and medication, you should agree to be confined to a hospital. Here, you will receive adequate care and attention. You will also be encouraged to seek social support within your community.

Remember that you may be a hazard to yourself and others if you become uncontrollable, which is why you need to consider hospitalization if you find yourself no longer responding to medication. If you need immediate crisis intervention, you may be admitted to an emergency room. Crisis management is actually an integral part of borderline personality disorder treatment.

Conclusion

Thank you again for downloading this book!

I hope this book was able to help you learn more about borderline personality disorder!

The next step is to put the strategies provided into use, and begin improving your personality disorder!

Finally, if you enjoyed this book, please take the time to share your thoughts and post a review on Amazon. It'd be greatly appreciated!

Thank you and good luck!

www.ingramcontent.com/pod-product-compliance
Lightning Source LLC
LaVergne TN
LVHW021748060526
838200LV00052B/3535